Appaloosa
Zebra

APPALOOSA ZEBRA

A HORSE LOVER'S ALPHABET

By **Jessie Haas**

Pictures by **Margot Apple**

Greenwillow Books, *An Imprint of* HarperCollins Publishers

For Andrea Chin
and Leia Robinson
— J. H.

For Jessie and Susan
— M. A.

The following was a valuable source of
horse breed information for this book: *The
Encyclopedia of the Horse* by Elwyn Hartly
Edwards (New York: Dorling Kindersley, 1994).

Appaloosa Zebra: A Horse Lover's Alphabet
Text copyright © 2002 by Jessie Haas
Illustrations copyright © 2002 by Margot Apple
All rights reserved. Printed in Singapore by Tien Wah Press.
www.harperchildrens.com

Colored pencils were used for the full-color art.
The text type is Lemonade.

Library of Congress Cataloging-in-Publication Data
Haas, Jessie.
Appaloosa zebra: a horse lover's alphabet /
by Jessie Haas; illustrated by Margot Apple.
        p.   cm.
"Greenwillow Books."
Summary: Moving through the alphabet, a girl ponders
the many different kinds of horses she will have when
she gets older, from Appaloosa to zebra.
ISBN 0-688-17880-4 (trade). ISBN 0-688-17881-2 (lib. bdg.)
[Horses—Fiction. 2. Alphabet] I. Apple, Margot, ill. II. Title.
PZ7.H1128 Ap 2002   [E]—dc21   00-048437

10   9   8   7   6   5   4   3   2   1
First Edition

When I'm older, I'll have a horse farm.
All kinds of horses will live with me.

Spotted **A**ppaloosas.

Arabian steeds.

A big blond Belgian will be my buddy.
I'll brush him and bridle him and
ride him bareback.

I'll have a Connemara
and a couple of Clydesdales.

One of the Clydesdales will be a colt.

I'll call my darling Donkey Dobbin.
I'll drive him in a dogcart to go to
the dump.

Eventually I'll have every kind of horse. I'd have an **E**ohippus if they weren't extinct.

My **F**jord pony will be fat and frisky.
The farrier will take care of his feet.

Then I'll **G**room him and get on
and gallop and gallop.

On hot summer days I'll put
on my hard hat, hop on my
Haflinger, go for a hack.

My **I**rish hunter will be immense.
In **J**odhpurs and jacket
I'll joyfully
jump.

I'll keep on winning
the **K**entucky Derby.

My **L**ipizzans will perform

lively leaps,

the lightest of lengthenings,

lovely levades.

On my farm I'll have a multitude of **M**organs and a mouse-colored mule.

My horses will Neigh whenever they see me. They'll nicker and nuzzle and never ever nip.

Old police horses, under the oak tree, will eat their Oats and dream their dreams.

Peruvian Pasos and palomino ponies will play in the paddock and prance in parades.

My Quarter horse will be quick and quiet. She'll be quite good at reining, and she'll herd cattle, too.

cutting a calf from the herd

Racing and rodeos, roping and
roundups: I'll ride and I'll ride
and I'll ride and I'll ride.

reining

spin

sliding stop

barrel racing

calf roping

In my stable I'll have a small Shetland and a sizable Shire.

My Trotters and Thoroughbreds will travel to the tracks. I'll need a truck and a trailer and some big tack trunks.

Usually **U**nicorns lurk unseen.
Mine will be unconventionally bold.

I'll be a **V**aquera.

I'll do a lot
of vaulting.

I'll ride my white **W**elsh pony Western.

Xenophon wrote the first text about horses. I'll examine it often for expert advice.

Yippee-yi-yay! I'll yelp and
I'll yodel out on the tundra
as I round up my Yakuts.

A dozen Zebras in zigzag stripes
will graze in my pasture and dazzle
my friends.

Appaloosa to **Z**ebra, my farm is all planned.
Every day I get older. Oh, I can't wait!

MORE ABOUT HORSES

Eohippus, the earliest ancestor of the horse, lived 60 million years ago. She was as tall as a collie dog, and she had toes: four on her front feet and three on her back.

Horses, **donkeys**, and **zebras** all descended from eohippus. Zebras live wild in Africa. Donkeys live all over the world and were tamed before horses.

If you breed a horse to a donkey you get a **mule**. Mules have long ears like donkeys and make the same sound: *Heee-haww!* Mules are as big as their horse mothers. They are stronger than horses and very, very stubborn.

A baby horse is called a **colt** if it's a boy and a filly if it's a girl. (If you don't know which, call it a foal.)

Ever since horses were first tamed, people have been thinking about the best way to handle them. **Xenophon**, a Greek general, wrote his ideas down about 2,400 years ago, and they still make sense. Horses and people haven't changed much in all that time.

Unlike eohippus, horses have only one toe.

It's called a hoof, and it's mostly toenail. A **farrier** trims a horse's hooves and hammers on shoes. (It doesn't hurt the horse, just as it doesn't hurt you to cut your fingernail—unless you cut it too short.)

There are hundreds of kinds of horses in the world. They come in three basic sizes.

A **pony** is a small horse. Ponies are shorter than 58 inches, measured to the highest part of the back. There are many breeds of pony. **Connemaras** are famous for being good jumpers. They come from Ireland. **Welsh ponies** from Wales are great riding ponies, fast and agile. **Fjord ponies** from Norway look like the horses in cave paintings. They're big enough for grown-ups to ride and strong enough for farm work. So are **Haflingers**, golden ponies with blond manes and tails that come from Austria. **Shetland ponies** are the smallest ponies. They come from the cold and stony Shetland Islands of Scotland.

Draft horses are large horses used to pull heavy loads. Their ancestors were ridden by knights, who needed strong horses to carry them in their armor. **Belgians** are big, broad, heavy draft horses from Belgium. **Clydesdales** are tall, long-legged, high-stepping draft horses from Scotland. **Shires** are taller than Clydesdales and heavier than Belgians. They are the biggest horses in the world, and come from England.

Saddle horses and harness horses are taller than ponies and lighter than draft horses. **Trotters race** at a trot, pulling a light cart. **Thoroughbreds** are the fastest racehorses in the world. The most famous Thoroughbred race in the United States is the **Kentucky Derby. Quarter horses** are fast, too, for about a quarter of a mile; that's how they got their name. They're great at **herding** cattle and at **reining**, a modern sport with lots of galloping, fast stops, and spins.

Peruvian Pasos from Peru have gaits so smooth that you could ride one carrying a full glass of water and not spill a drop. **Irish hunters** are half Thoroughbred, half Irish draft horse, and are bred for fox hunting. **Morgans** were developed in New England to be all-purpose horses. They did farmwork, carried people to town in buggies and under saddle, and raced. Morgans are still great family horses.

Some horses can live in extreme climates. The **Yakut pony** lives in Siberia, north of the Arctic Circle. Yakuts are short, white, and very hairy. **Arabians** come from the Arabian desert. Arabians are beautiful, spirited saddle horses with a thin, smooth coat. (**Steed** is another

word for a fine horse.) Many Arabians are white, like Yakuts. In the desert, white animals stay cooler. In the Arctic, white animals blend in with the snow, so wolves and bears can't see them easily.

Horses come from all over the world. **Appaloosas**, from the American West, carried the Nez Perce on buffalo hunts. Appaloosas have spots.

The Spanish Riding School in Vienna, Austria, is the world's oldest riding academy. There, **Lipizzan** horses learn to dance, to trot in place, and to perform difficult **leaps. Lengthening** means making the stride long and impressive. The **levade** is when the horse rears and freezes, holding the pose for almost half a minute.

Palomino is a color, seen in many different breeds. Palominos are golden, with light blond manes and tails.

Unicorns live in fairy tales and folktales. They have a spiral horn growing from their foreheads, and they're shy.

Unlike you, horses have four legs. They can move them at different speeds and in different sequences. The different speeds and sequences are called gaits. Walking is the slowest gait. It sounds like 1-2-3-4, 1-2-3-4. (Make the sound on a desk by tapping your fingers.) The trot is the medium gait: 1-2, 1-2, 1-2. The canter is faster: 1-2-3, 1-2-3, 1-2-3. The **gallop** is the

fastest gait: 1-2-3-4, 1-2-3-4, 1-2-3-4, like the walk only much quicker.

A **stable** is a horse barn. A **paddock** is a fenced area near the stable where horses can **graze**, which means *to eat grass*. Horses also like **oats**. They greet a friend or their dinner with a loud cry called a **neigh** or a low chuckling sound called a **nicker**. They **nuzzle** by pushing gently with their noses. You **groom** them by cleaning them with a brush.

Then you get ready to go for a drive. Maybe you'll take the **dogcart**. It's a one-horse cart that holds two people, sitting back to back.

Instead of driving you might go for a **hack**, a pleasant easygoing ride. First you'd have to put on the **tack**—the saddle and bridle. The **bridle** goes on the horse's head. The reins, connected to the bit in the horse's mouth, let a rider steer and stop the horse. Saddles come in English and **Western** styles. In the Southwest, if you're a **vaquera** (a cowgirl) or a vaquero (a cowboy), you wear Western clothes—cowboy boots and hat, and blue jeans. Over your jeans you might wear chaps— leather pants to protect your legs from brush. If you ride English style, you wear a **hard hat**

to protect your head, in case you fall off while jumping, and you wear riding pants called **jodhpurs** and a **jacket**.

If you're really adventurous, you'll do some **vaulting**. Then you won't use a saddle at all, just a strap to hold onto while you do gymnastics at full gallop.

Be careful! And have fun!